Devotional For Dating Christian Couples

42 WEEKLY DEVOTIONS TO GROW CLOSER TO GOD AND EACH OTHER

DIANA HARTLEY

TABLE OF CONTENTS

About This Book

"*Devotional for Dating Christian Couples*" is a guidebook designed to help Christian dating couples strengthen their relationship with God and each other. This book features 42 devotions that can be used once a week, each designed to help couples grow closer to God and one another. The book also includes guidance on using it effectively and creating a devotional routine that works for you and your partner.

Why Devotions are Important for Christian Dating Couples

As a Christian dating couple, my husband and I knew the importance of building our relationship on a foundation of faith. However, we found it challenging to find ways to consistently grow in our faith together. That is until we discovered the power of devotion.

At first, we struggled to create a routine that worked for both of us. We tried doing devotions in the morning but found it difficult to wake up early enough to make it work. We tried doing them in the evening, but often found ourselves too tired or distracted to fully engage. It wasn't until we committed to doing devotions once a week, on Sunday afternoons, that we found a routine that worked for us.

Our first few devotions were a bit awkward as we tried to figure out what to do and say. But over time, we began to look forward to our weekly devotional time as a way to connect with God. We found that it helped us to have a shared experience of growing in our faith, and it provided a space for us to discuss the challenges and joys of our relationship in a meaningful way.

As we continued to do devotions together, we noticed a change in our relationship. We became more intentional about putting God first in our relationship, and we learned to communicate with each other more openly and honestly. We found that devotions helped us to stay grounded in our faith, even during difficult times in our relationship.

Looking back, we realize that devotions were a critical part of our dating relationship. They helped us to grow closer to each other and God, and they provided a foundation for our marriage. We continue to do devotions together as a married couple, and we are grateful for the impact that they have had on our relationship. We would encourage any Christian dating couple to make devotion a priority in their relationship – it truly makes a difference.

How to Use This Book

This book is designed to be used as a weekly devotional guide for Christian dating couples. Here are some tips on how to use this book effectively:

- **How to Create a Devotional Routine**

To create a devotional routine, it is important to find a time and place that works for both partners. Some couples prefer to do devotions in the morning, while others prefer the evening. It's important to find a consistent time that works for both partners so that devotions become a regular part of your routine. Additionally, finding a quiet and distraction-free place to do devotions can help you to focus and connect with God.

- **Tips for a Successful Devotional Time**

To have a successful devotional time, it's important to approach it with a positive attitude and an open heart. Make sure to turn off all distractions, such as phones and computers, and give your full attention to the devotion. It can also be helpful to take notes and reflect on the devotion afterward. Finally, it's important to approach devotions as a team, working together to learn and grow in your faith.

Part One

Foundation of Faith

In this section, we will focus on the foundation of faith that is essential for a strong and healthy relationship. As Christian dating couples, it is important to build our relationship on a solid foundation of faith in God. This foundation will provide the strength and support that we need to navigate the challenges of dating and prepare us for a lifelong commitment to each other. In this section, we will explore key aspects of building a strong foundation of faith, including prayer, Bible study, and worship. So let's dive in and explore how we can strengthen our relationship with God and with each other.

WEEK 1

God's Design for Relationships

"So God created man in his own image, in the image of God he created him; male and female he created them."

Genesis 1:27 (ESV)

Devotion:

As Christian dating couples, we know that God has a purpose and plan for our lives, including our relationships. From the very beginning, God created us in His image and designed us for a relationship with Him and with each other. As we seek to honor God in our dating relationship, it's important to understand His design for relationships.

God created us as unique individuals, with our strengths and weaknesses. He also created us to be in a relationship with one another. In a dating relationship, it's important to honor each other's individuality and to appreciate the differences that make us unique.

At the same time, God created us male and female, with distinct roles and responsibilities. As we seek to honor God in our dating relationship, it's important to understand and respect the roles that God has given us. This means treating each other with respect and kindness and seeking to build each other up in our faith and our relationship.

PRAYER

As we reflect on God's design for relationships, let's take a moment to pray for our dating relationship. Let's ask God to help us honor Him in all that we do, and to guide us as we seek to build a strong and healthy relationship. May we always seek to put God first in our relationship, and may we strive to live according to His design for our lives. Amen.

WEEK 2

Trusting God's Timing

"For everything, there is a season, and a time for every matter under heaven"

Ecclesiastes 3:1 (ESV)

Devotion:

We often find ourselves wondering about the future of our relationship. We may ask questions like "When will we get engaged?" or "When will we get married?" While it's natural to have these questions, it's important to remember that God's timing is perfect. He knows the plans that He has for us, and He will guide us in His perfect timing.

In Ecclesiastes 3:1, we read that there is a time for everything. This includes a time for dating, a time for engagement, and a time for marriage. We may not always understand why God is leading us in a certain direction, but we can trust that His plans for us are good.

Trusting in God's timing can be difficult, especially when we feel like we're ready for the next step in our relationship. But we must remember that God sees the big picture, and He knows what's best for us. When we trust in Him, we can have confidence that He will lead us in the right direction.

PRAYER

As we reflect on trusting God's timing in our dating relationship, let's take a moment to pray. Let's ask God to help us trust in His plans for us, even when we don't understand. May we have patience and faith as we wait for His perfect timing. And may we continue to seek Him first in our relationship, trusting that He will guide us every step of the way. Amen.

WEEK 3

Pursuing Purity

"Blessed are the pure in heart, for they shall see God."

Matthew 5:8 (ESV)

Devotion:

As Christian dating couples, we are called to pursue purity in all areas of our lives. This includes our thoughts, words, and actions, as well as our physical purity. God's desire for us is to live a life that honors Him and reflects His holiness.

Pursuing purity requires discipline and self-control. It means making intentional choices that align with God's will for our lives, even when those choices may be difficult or unpopular. It also means seeking accountability and support from fellow believers who can help us stay on track.

In Matthew 5:8, Jesus teaches us that the pure in heart will see God. As we seek to honor God in our dating relationship, let's strive to pursue purity in all areas of our lives. Let's ask God to give us the strength and self-control that we need to make choices that honor Him, and to surround us with supportive friends who will help us stay accountable. May we always remember that pursuing purity is not just about following a set of rules, but about living a life that reflects God's love and holiness.

PRAYER

Heavenly Father, we thank you for your love and your desire for us to live a life of purity. Help us to make choices that honor you and to seek accountability and support from those around us. Give us the strength and self-control that we need to pursue purity in all areas of our lives, and help us to reflect our holiness to the world around us. Amen.

WEEK 4

The Power of Prayer

"Therefore I tell you, whatever you ask in prayer, believe that you have received it, and it will be yours."

Mark 11:24 (ESV)

Devotion:

As Christian dating couples, we know the power of prayer. Prayer is our direct line of communication with God, and it's through prayer that we can seek His guidance, wisdom, and provision in all areas of our lives, including our dating relationship.

In Mark 11:24, Jesus tells us that whatever we ask for in prayer, we should believe that we have received it, and it will be ours. This doesn't mean that we will always receive exactly what we ask for, but it does mean that God hears our prayers and will answer them according to His will and timing.

As we seek to honor God in our dating relationship, let's make prayer a priority. Let's take time each day to pray together, seeking God's guidance and wisdom in our relationship. Let's also pray individually, asking God to reveal His will for our lives and to help us grow in our relationship with Him.

PRAYER

As we reflect on the power of prayer, let's take a moment to pray together. Let's thank God for His love and faithfulness, and for the privilege of being able to come before Him in prayer. Let's ask Him to guide us as we seek to honor Him in our dating relationship, and to give us the faith and trust that we need to believe that He will answer our prayers according to His will and timing. May prayer be the foundation of our relationship with God and with each other. Amen.

WEEK 5

Growing in Christlikeness

"But grow in the grace and knowledge of our Lord and Savior Jesus Christ. To him be the glory both now and to the day of eternity. Amen."

2 Peter 3:18 (ESV)

Devotion:

As Christian dating couples, one of our greatest desires should be to grow in Christlikeness. This means becoming more like Jesus in our thoughts, words, and actions, and seeking to live a life that honors God and reflects His love to the world around us.

Growing in Christlikeness requires intentional effort and a commitment to following Jesus. It means spending time in God's Word, seeking His guidance and wisdom in prayer, and being open to the leading of the Holy Spirit in our lives. It also means being willing to make changes and adjustments in our lives as we seek to align our hearts with God's will.

In 2 Peter 3:18, we are called to "grow in the grace and knowledge of our Lord and Savior Jesus Christ." As we seek to honor God in our dating relationship, let's make it our goal to grow in Christlikeness each day. Let's ask God to give us the strength and wisdom that we need to follow Jesus faithfully, and to help us reflect His love and grace to the world around us.

PRAYER

Heavenly Father, we thank you for your love and your desire for us to grow in Christlikeness. Help us to follow Jesus faithfully and to seek your guidance and wisdom in all areas of our lives. Give us the strength and courage that we need to make changes and adjustments in our lives as we seek to honor you. May we reflect your love and grace to the world around us as we grow in Christlikeness. Amen.

WEEK 6

Honoring God with Your Bodies

"Or do you not know that your body is a temple of the Holy Spirit within you, whom you have from God? You are not your own, for you were bought with a price. So glorify God in your body."

1 Corinthians 6:19-20 (ESV)

Devotion:

As Christian dating couples, we are called to honor God with our bodies. This means treating our bodies with respect and care and avoiding anything that would dishonor God or harm ourselves or others. It also means recognizing that our bodies are temples of the Holy Spirit and that we have been bought with a price through the sacrifice of Jesus on the cross.

Honoring God with our bodies requires discipline and self-control. It means making intentional choices that align with God's will for our lives, even when those choices may be difficult or unpopular. It also means seeking accountability and support from fellow believers who can help us stay on track.

In 1 Corinthians 6:19-20, we are reminded that our bodies are not our own, but have been bought with a price. As we seek to honor God in our dating relationship, let's make it our goal to honor Him with our bodies in every way. Let's ask God to give us the strength and self-control that we need to make choices that honor Him, and to surround us with supportive friends who will help us stay accountable. May we always remember that honoring God with our bodies is not just about following a set of rules, but about living a life that reflects His love and holiness.

PRAYER

Dear Lord, we thank you for your love and your desire for us to honor you with our bodies. Help us to make choices that honor you and to seek accountability and support from those around us. Give us the strength and self-control that we need to honor you with our bodies in every way, and help us to remember that our bodies are not our own, but have been bought with a price through the sacrifice of Jesus on the cross. May we always seek to glorify you in our bodies and our dating relationship. Amen.

WEEK 7

Putting God First

"But seek first the kingdom of God and his righteousness, and all these things will be added to you."

Matthew 6:33 (ESV)

Devotion:

It can be easy to get caught up in our desires and plans for our dating relationship. But as Christians, we are called to put God first in everything we do, including our relationships.

In Matthew 6:33, Jesus tells us to seek God's kingdom and righteousness above all else and promises that when we do, everything else will fall into place. When we prioritize our relationship with God, we will see the fruit of His blessings in every area of our lives, including our dating relationship.

Putting God first means seeking His guidance and wisdom in all of our decisions, including our relationships. It means praying together, studying God's

Word together, and seeking to honor Him in every aspect of our relationship. When we do this, we will experience a deeper level of intimacy and trust in our relationship with each other, as well as with God.

Let's make it our priority to seek God first in our relationship and trust Him to guide us in the right direction. Let's pray for His wisdom and guidance as we seek to honor Him in everything we do, including our dating relationship.

PRAYER

Dear God, we thank you for your love and faithfulness towards us. Help us to put you first in our relationship, and to seek your guidance and wisdom in everything we do. Give us the strength and courage to follow your will for our lives, and to honor you in every aspect of our relationship. May your love and grace guide us as we seek to grow closer to you and each other. Amen.

Part Two

Communication and Conflict

In this section, we will explore the important topics of communication and conflict in relationships. Communication is the key to building healthy relationships, and conflict is an inevitable part of any relationship. As Christian couples, we must learn how to communicate effectively and handle conflict in a way that honors God and strengthens our relationship. Let's dive into these important topics and discover how we can communicate better and handle conflict in a way that pleases God.

WEEK 8

Learning to Listen

"Let every person be quick to hear, slow to speak, slow to anger."

James 1:19 (ESV)

Devotion:

One of the most important aspects of communication is listening. Yet, listening is often the most difficult part of communication. We tend to be quick to speak and slow to listen. However, as Christian dating couples, we must learn to listen if we want to build healthy and strong relationships.

In James 1:19, we are reminded to be "quick to hear, slow to speak, slow to anger." This means that we should make a conscious effort to listen carefully to what the other person is saying before we respond. We should seek to understand their perspective and try to put ourselves in their shoes.

Learning to listen requires patience, humility, and self-control. It means being willing to set aside our agendas and desires for the sake of the other person. When we listen to others, we show them that we value and respect them.

Let's make it a habit to practice listening in our dating relationship. Let's be quick to hear and slow to speak, just as James 1:19 instructs us. By doing so, we can build deeper connections with each other and grow in our love for one another.

PRAYER

Dear God, help us to be better listeners in our dating relationship. Teach us to be patient, humble, and self-controlled as we seek to understand each other. May our hearts be open to one another, and may we show each other the love and respect that we deserve. Help us to grow closer to each other as we learn to listen more effectively. Amen.

WEEK 9

Speaking the Truth in Love

"Rather, speaking the truth in love, we are to grow up in every way into him who is the head, into Christ."

Ephesians 4:15 (ESV)

Devotion:

Communication is key in any relationship, but it's especially important in a dating relationship where you are getting to know each other on a deeper level. It's important, to be honest and open with each other, but it's equally important to speak the truth in love.

In Ephesians 4:15, we are called to "speak the truth in love." This means that we should communicate honestly and openly with each other, but we should do so in a way that is kind, gentle, and loving. We should seek to build each other up, not tear each other down, and we should always be mindful of the impact our words can have on our partner.

As we seek to communicate with each other in our dating relationship, let's make it our goal to speak the truth in love. Let's be honest and open with each other, but let's do so in a way that is kind, gentle, and loving. Let's seek to build each other up and encourage each other, and let's always be mindful of the impact our words can have.

PRAYER

Heavenly Father, we thank you for the gift of communication and for the opportunity to get to know each other on a deeper level. Help us to speak the truth in love, always seeking to build each other up and encourage each other. Give us the wisdom and discernment that we need to communicate effectively and to be mindful of the impact our words can have. May our communication be a reflection of your love and grace, and may it bring us closer to each other and you. Amen.

WEEK 10

Forgiveness and Reconciliation

"For if you forgive others their trespasses, your heavenly Father will also forgive you, but if you do not forgive others their trespasses, neither will your Father forgive your trespasses."

Matthew 6:14-15 (ESV)

Devotion:

Forgiveness is one of the cornerstones of our Christian faith. As we seek to follow Jesus, we are called to forgive others just as He has forgiven us. In our dating relationships, forgiveness and reconciliation are crucial for maintaining a healthy and thriving connection with our partner.

It can be difficult to forgive when we have been hurt or wronged, but the Bible reminds us that forgiveness is necessary for our well-being and our relationship with God. In Matthew 6:14-15, Jesus teaches us that if we forgive others, our Heavenly Father will also forgive us.

But if we do not forgive others, then we will not receive forgiveness ourselves.

When we choose to forgive, we release the burden of anger, bitterness, and resentment that we may be carrying. We also create space for reconciliation and healing in our relationships. This does not mean that we should forget what has happened or that we will never feel the pain of the hurt again, but it does mean that we choose to let go of the offense and move forward in love and grace.

PRAYER

Heavenly Father, we thank you for your example of forgiveness and reconciliation. Help us to follow your lead and to forgive others just as you have forgiven us. Give us the strength and courage to let go of our anger, bitterness, and resentment, and to extend grace and love to those who have hurt us. May our relationships be characterized by forgiveness and reconciliation, and may we reflect your love and grace to the world around us. Amen.

WEEK 11

Overcoming Conflict

"Blessed are the peacemakers, for they shall be called sons of God."

Matthew 5:9 (ESV)

Devotion:

Conflict is a natural part of any relationship, but it can be especially challenging in a dating relationship. Disagreements and misunderstandings can easily lead to hurt feelings and damaged trust, making it difficult to move forward and grow closer to one another.

As followers of Jesus, we are called to be peacemakers. In Matthew 5:9, Jesus teaches that "blessed are the peacemakers, for they shall be called sons of God." This means that when we work to resolve conflict and promote peace in our relationships, we are reflecting God's character and bringing glory to His name.

When conflict arises in our dating relationship, it can be tempting to avoid the issue or to try to "win" the argument. But as Christians, we are called to a higher standard. We are called to speak the truth in love, to seek forgiveness and reconciliation when we have hurt one another, and to work together to overcome conflict.

Let's make it our goal to be peacemakers in our dating relationship. Let's seek to listen to one another, speak the truth in love, and work together to find solutions that honor God and strengthen our relationship. And let's always remember that God is with us, guiding us and giving us the strength that we need to overcome conflict and promote peace.

PRAYER

Dear God, we thank you for your love and your desire for us to be peacemakers in our relationships. Help us to listen to one another, to speak the truth in love, and to work together to overcome conflict. Give us the wisdom and strength that we need to promote peace and reconciliation in our dating relationship, and to reflect your character to the world around us. Amen.

WEEK 12

Building Healthy Boundaries

"Above all else, guard your heart, for everything you do flows from it."

Proverbs 4:23 (ESV)

Devotion:

As Christian dating couples, it's important to build healthy boundaries in our relationships. Boundaries help us to protect our hearts and honor God in our actions and choices. When we have clear boundaries, we can prevent harmful behaviors and conflicts, and build a strong foundation for a healthy and fulfilling relationship.

Proverbs 4:23 says, "Above all else, guard your heart, for everything you do flows from it." Our hearts are precious to God, and He desires for us to protect them from harm. This means setting boundaries that honor our values, beliefs, and convictions, and that help us to grow in our relationship with God and each other.

Building healthy boundaries requires open communication and a willingness to work together as a team. We need to be honest with ourselves and with each other about our needs and expectations, and be willing to make compromises and adjustments as needed. We also need to be respectful and considerate of each other's feelings and emotions and seek to honor God in our actions and choices.

PRAYER

Our Father, we thank you for your love and guidance in our relationship. Help us to build healthy boundaries that honor you and protect our hearts. Give us the wisdom and strength that we need to communicate openly and honestly with each other, and to work together as a team. May we always seek to honor you in our actions and choices, and grow in our love for you and each other. In Jesus' name, we pray, Amen.

WEEK 13

Resolving Differences with Grace

"Bearing with one another and, if one has a complaint against another, forgiving each other; as the Lord has forgiven you, so you also must forgive."

Colossians 3:13 (ESV)

Devotion:

As human beings, it's natural for us to have differences and disagreements with the people we love, even in our dating relationships. However, as Christians, we are called to approach these differences with grace and forgiveness, just as the Lord has forgiven us.

In Colossians 3:13, we are reminded to "bear with one another and, if one has a complaint against another, forgive each other; as the Lord has forgiven you, so you also must forgive." This is not always easy, but it is essential if we want to maintain healthy relationships and honor God in our interactions with others.

Resolving differences with grace means approaching the situation with a spirit of humility and a desire to understand the other person's perspective. It means listening actively and seeking to find common ground, rather than just pushing our agenda. And it means being willing to forgive, even when it's difficult because we know that God has forgiven us.

PRAYER

Dear Lord, we thank you for your grace and forgiveness, and we ask for your help in extending that same grace and forgiveness to the people in our lives, especially our dating partner. Give us the strength and wisdom that we need to approach differences and disagreements with humility and a desire for understanding. Help us to listen actively and to seek common ground, and to be willing to forgive, even when it's difficult. May we reflect your love and grace in all of our interactions with others. Amen.

WEEK 14

The Art of Apology

"So if you are offering your gift at the altar and there remember that your brother has something against you, leave your gift there before the altar and go. First, be reconciled to your brother, and then come and offer your gift."

Matthew 5:23-24 (ESV)

Devotion:

One of the most important aspects of any healthy relationship is the ability to apologize when we have hurt someone else. Apologizing takes humility, courage, and a willingness to acknowledge our mistakes and seek forgiveness.

In Matthew 5:23-24, Jesus teaches us the importance of reconciliation and making things right with others. He says that if we remember that someone has something against us, we should leave our offering at the altar and go be reconciled to that person first.

When we apologize to someone, we are not only seeking their forgiveness, but we are also acknowledging that we value our relationship with them and want to make things right. This is especially important in dating relationships, where misunderstandings and disagreements can easily arise.

As we seek to cultivate healthy relationships, let's commit to practicing the art of apology. Let's be quick to admit our mistakes and seek forgiveness, and let's extend grace and forgiveness to others when they apologize to us.

PRAYER

Dear God, thank You for the gift of relationships and the opportunity to love and serve others. Help us to be humble and courageous as we seek to apologize to those we have hurt. Give us the wisdom to know when we need to seek reconciliation, and the grace to extend forgiveness to others. May our relationships be marked by love, grace, and a willingness to apologize and seek forgiveness when needed. In Jesus' name, amen.

Part Three

Building a Christ-Centered Relationship

In this section, we will focus on building a Christ-centered relationship. As we strive to honor God in our dating relationship, we must keep Jesus at the center of all that we do. In this section, we will explore what it means to build a relationship that is rooted in Christ and how we can navigate the ups and downs of dating with faith and intentionality.

WEEK 15

Unity in Christ

"I appeal to you, brothers, by the name of our Lord Jesus Christ, that all of you agree, and that there be no divisions among you, but that you be united in the same mind and the same judgment."

1 Corinthians 1:10 (ESV)

Devotion:

As Christian dating couples, our relationship should be centered around Christ. This means seeking to grow in our faith together, pursuing unity, and striving to honor God in all that we do.

In 1 Corinthians 1:10, Paul appeals to the Corinthian believers to be united in Christ, to agree with one another, and to have the same mind and judgment. This call to unity is just as relevant for us today as it was for the early church.

Unity doesn't mean that we always agree on everything or that we never have disagreements or conflicts.

Rather, it means that we approach our relationship with a spirit of humility, seeking to understand each other's perspectives, and prioritizing our love and commitment to Christ above all else.

As we strive to build a Christ-centered relationship, let's make it our goal to pursue unity in all things. Let's commit to seeking God's guidance and wisdom in our relationship, and to putting His will above our desires and preferences. May our love for Christ and our commitment to His Word be the foundation of our unity, and may we always seek to honor Him in all that we do.

PRAYER

Heavenly Father, we thank you for the gift of unity in Christ. Help us to approach our relationship with a spirit of humility, seeking to understand each other's perspectives, and prioritizing our love for You above all else. Guide us by Your Holy Spirit and help us to make decisions that honor You and build up our relationship. May our love for you be the foundation of our unity, and may we always seek to honor you in all that we do. Amen.

WEEK 16

Serving Together

"For even the Son of Man came not to be served but to serve, and to give his life as a ransom for many."

Mark 10:45 (ESV)

Devotion:

As we seek to build a Christ-centered relationship, one important aspect is serving together. Jesus Himself set the example for us when He came to earth not to be served but to serve others and give His life as a ransom for many (Mark 10:45).

Serving together as a couple can take many forms, whether it's volunteering at a local charity, participating in a mission trip, or simply serving our friends and family in practical ways. Whatever it may be, serving together can strengthen our relationship and help us grow in our faith.

As we serve others, we not only bless those around us, but we also grow in humility and learn to put the needs of others before our own. It's a beautiful way to reflect the love of Christ to the world and to live out the Gospel in tangible ways.

Let's make serving others a priority in our relationship and ask God to guide us in finding ways to serve together. May we follow Jesus' example of selflessness and put others first as we seek to build a Christ-centered relationship.

PRAYER

Dear God, we are grateful for the example of Jesus, who came to serve and give His life for us. Help us to follow His example and to serve others with humility and selflessness. Guide us as we seek to find ways to serve together as a couple and bless those around us. May our love for you and others grow as we serve together and build a Christ-centered relationship. In Jesus' name, amen.

WEEK 17

Sharing Your Testimonies

"But in your hearts honor Christ the Lord as holy, always being prepared to make a defense to anyone who asks you for a reason for the hope that is in you; yet do it with gentleness and respect."

1 Peter 3:15 (ESV)

Devotion:

As Christians, we have been saved by grace through faith in Jesus Christ. Our salvation is a gift from God, and it is something that we should be grateful for every day. As we grow in our relationship with Christ, we are called to share our testimonies with others and to be prepared to give a reason for the hope that we have in Jesus.

Sharing our testimonies can be a powerful way to share the love and grace of Jesus with others. It allows us to share how God has worked in our lives, and how He has brought us through difficult times. It also allows us to share how God has transformed our hearts and minds, and how He has given us a new perspective on life.

In 1 Peter 3:15, we are called to "always be prepared to make a defense to anyone who asks you for a reason for the hope that is in you." Let's make it our goal to share our testimonies with others, and to be ready to give a reason for the hope that we have in Jesus.

PRAYER

Dear Father, we thank you for the gift of salvation through faith in Jesus Christ. Help us to grow in our relationship with you, and to be prepared to share our testimonies with others. Give us the words to speak, and the courage to share our faith with those around us. May our testimonies be powerful witness to your love and grace, and may they bring others to know you as their Lord and Savior. Amen.

WEEK 18

Celebrating God's Gifts

"Every good gift and every perfect gift is from above, coming down from the Father of lights, with whom there is no variation or shadow due to change."

James 1:17 (ESV)

Devotion:

In our dating relationships, it's important to recognize and celebrate the gifts that God has given us. These gifts can come in many different forms - from the people that God has placed in our lives, to the talents and abilities that He has given us, to the opportunities that we have to serve and make a difference in the world.

As we seek to build a Christ-centered relationship, let's take time to reflect on the gifts that God has given us, and to thank Him for His goodness and faithfulness in our lives. Let's also commit to using these gifts for His glory, and to using our relationship to serve and bless others.

In James 1:17, we are reminded that "every good gift and every perfect gift is from above, coming down from the Father of lights." Let's take time to thank God for the gifts that He has given us, and to seek His guidance and wisdom as we use these gifts to honor Him.

PRAYER

Dear Lord, we thank you for the many gifts that you have given us. We thank You for the people that You have placed in our lives, for the talents and abilities that You have given us, and for the opportunities that we have to serve and make a difference in the world. Help us to use these gifts for your glory, and to honor you in our relationship. Give us wisdom and guidance as we seek to build a Christ-centered relationship, and help us to celebrate your goodness and faithfulness in our lives. Amen.

WEEK 19

Being a Witness to Others

"But you will receive power when the Holy Spirit has come upon you, and you will be my witnesses in Jerusalem and in all Judea and Samaria, and to the end of the earth."

Acts 1:8 (ESV)

Devotion:

As Christians, we are called to be witnesses to the world around us, sharing the good news of Jesus Christ with those who do not yet know Him. This call to witness is not just for pastors and missionaries but for every believer.

In Acts 1:8, Jesus tells His disciples that they will receive power when the Holy Spirit comes upon them, and they will be His witnesses "in Jerusalem and all Judea and Samaria, and to the end of the earth." This same call to be witnesses applies to us today, wherever we are and whatever we do.

In our dating relationships, we have a unique opportunity to be witnesses to our partner and those around us. We can show the love and grace of Jesus in the way we treat our partner, in the way we handle conflicts, and in the way we serve others together.

Let's make it our goal to be intentional about sharing our faith with our partner and those around us. Let's ask God to give us the courage and wisdom to be bold witnesses for Him, and to help us live in a way that reflects His love and grace.

PRAYER

Heavenly Father, we thank you for the opportunity to be witnesses for you. Help us to be intentional about sharing our faith with our partner and those around us. Give us the courage and wisdom to be bold witnesses for you, and help us to live in a way that reflects your love and grace. May our dating relationship be a testimony to your goodness and faithfulness. Amen.

WEEK 20

Supporting Each Other's Dreams

"Do nothing from rivalry or conceit, but in humility count others more significant than yourselves."

Philippians 2:3 (ESV)

Devotion:

As a couple, it's important to support each other's dreams and aspirations. God has given each of us unique gifts and talents, and He has a specific purpose and plan for our lives. As we seek to follow Him, we can trust that He will lead us and guide us in the path that He has for us.

However, it's easy to get caught up in our ambitions and desires and forget to support and encourage our partner. We may feel jealous or resentful when our partner is succeeding in an area where we are not, or we may be so focused on our own goals that we neglect to show interest and support for our partner's dreams.

In Philippians 2:3, we are reminded to "do nothing from rivalry or conceit, but in humility count others more significant than yourselves." This means putting aside our desires and ambitions and focusing on supporting and encouraging our partner. It means celebrating their successes and being there to pick them up when they face setbacks or obstacles.

Let's commit to supporting each other's dreams and aspirations. Let's pray for each other and ask God to give us the wisdom and discernment that we need to fulfill His plan for our lives. And let's always remember to put our trust in Him, knowing that He has good plans for our future.

PRAYER

Dear God, we thank you for the unique gifts and talents that you have given each of us. Help us to support and encourage each other as we seek to fulfill your plan for our lives. Give us the humility and wisdom that we need to put each other first, and to celebrate each other's successes. Help us to always trust in you and to seek your will above all else. Amen.

WEEK 21

Love That Lasts

"Love bears all things, believes all things, hopes all things, and endures all things."

1 Corinthians 13:7 (ESV)

Devotion:

As we come towards the end of our journey together as dating couples, we reflect on the importance of love that lasts. The kind of love that is described in 1 Corinthians 13:7, bears all things, believes all things, hopes all things, and endures all things.

True love is not just a feeling or an emotion, but it is an intentional choice that we make to love and commit ourselves to another person. It is a love that goes beyond our desires and seeks the best for the other person. It is a love that is patient and kind, not jealous or boastful or arrogant or rude. It is a love that does not seek its way but seeks to honor and serve the other person.

As we seek to build Christ-centered relationships, let us strive to love each other in the same way that Jesus loves us. Let us be patient and kind, and let us bear with each other through the challenges that we may face. Let us believe in each other's potential, and let us hope and pray for each other's success. And let us endure through the trials and difficulties of life, knowing that God's love for us never fails.

PRAYER

God our Heavenly Father, we thank you for the gift of love that you have given us. Help us to love each other in the same way that you love us - with a love that bears all things, believes all things, hopes all things, and endures all things. Give us the strength and grace that we need to honor and serve each other, and to support each other in our dreams and goals. May our love for each other reflect your love for us, and may it bring glory and honor to your name. Amen.

Part Four

Facing Challenges Together

As couples journey through life, they will inevitably face various challenges and obstacles that will test their love and commitment to each other. This part of this devotional series is designed to help us navigate these challenges together, drawing strength from God and each other. Through these devotions, we will be encouraged to face our challenges with courage, faith, and hope, knowing that God is with us every step of the way.

WEEK 22

Persevering Through Trials

"Not only that, but we rejoice in our sufferings, knowing that suffering produces endurance, and endurance produces character, and character produces hope, and hope does not put us to shame, because God's love has been poured into our hearts through the Holy Spirit who has been given to us."

Romans 5:3-5 (ESV)

Devotion:

As we journey through life, we will face trials and challenges that will test our faith and endurance. These difficulties may come in various forms such as health issues, financial setbacks, job loss, or even relational struggles. It is easy to feel overwhelmed and discouraged during such times, but God's Word reminds us that we can persevere through trials and come out stronger on the other side.

In Romans 5:3-5, we are told that suffering produces endurance, endurance produces character, and character produces hope. As we face challenges in our relationship, let's choose to hold onto hope and trust that God is working all things together for our good. Let's allow our trials to shape us into the kind of people who reflect Christ's love and character to the world around us.

As we persevere through trials, we can also draw comfort from knowing that we are not alone. God promises to be with us every step of the way and to give us the strength and courage that we need to endure. Let's cling to His promises and trust that He will see us through whatever challenges we may face.

PRAYER

Dear Lord, we thank you for your faithfulness and for your promise to be with us through every trial and challenge. Give us the strength and endurance that we need to persevere through difficult times, and help us to grow in character and hope as we do. May our love for you and each other deepen as we face challenges together. We trust in your goodness and faithfulness, and we know that you are working all things together for our good. Amen.

WEEK 23

Trusting God When You're Apart

"Trust in the LORD with all your heart, and do not lean on your own understanding. In all your ways acknowledge him, and he will make straight your paths."

Proverbs 3:5-6 (ESV)

Devotion:

Being apart from your partner can be one of the most challenging things to deal with in a relationship. Whether it's due to distance, work, or other commitments, it can be difficult to trust God and His plan when you're not together.

However, the Bible reminds us to trust in the Lord with all our heart and not to lean on our understanding. This means we can have faith that God is in control, even when we don't understand why we have to be apart. It also means acknowledging God in all our ways and seeking His guidance and wisdom as we navigate the challenges of being apart.

We can take comfort in the fact that God is with us always, no matter where we are or what we're going through. We can trust that He is working all things together for our good, even when we can't see the result.

Let's make it our goal to trust God when we're apart from our partner. Let's seek His guidance and wisdom, and let's have faith that He is with us always, guiding us along the way.

PRAYER

Heavenly Father, we come before you with grateful hearts, thanking you for your constant love and care for us. As we face the challenges of being apart from our partner, we ask that you would help us to trust you with all our heart and to seek your guidance and wisdom in all we do. Remind us that you are always with us and that you are working all things together for our good. Give us the strength and faith we need to persevere through these trials and help us to keep our focus on you. In Jesus' name, we pray, Amen.

WEEK 24

Coping with Temptation

"No temptation has overtaken you that is not common to man. God is faithful, and he will not let you be tempted beyond your ability, but with the temptation he will also provide the way of escape, that you may be able to endure it."

1 Corinthians 10:13 (ESV)

Devotion:

As Christians, we are not immune to temptation. We are warned in the Bible that we will face trials and temptations in this life. But the good news is that we have a faithful God who promises to provide a way out when we are tempted.

In 1 Corinthians 10:13, we read that "No temptation has overtaken you that is not common to man. God is faithful, and he will not let you be tempted beyond your ability, but with the temptation he will also provide the way of escape, that you may be able to endure it." This verse reminds us that we are not alone in our struggles and that God is always with us, ready to provide a way out when we are tempted.

When we are faced with temptation, we must remember to turn to God and ask for His help. We can pray for strength and wisdom, and ask Him to guide us away from temptation and toward righteousness. We can also rely on the support and encouragement of our Christian community, which can help us stay accountable and provide comfort in times of struggle.

Let us strive to be strong in the face of temptation, relying on God's faithfulness to provide a way out for us. And let us remember to encourage and support one another as we journey through this life together.

PRAYER

Dear Lord, we thank you for your faithfulness and your promise to provide a way out when we are tempted. Give us the strength and wisdom to resist temptation and to follow your will in all things. Help us to rely on you and to seek the support of our Christian community when we are faced with trials and temptations. May we honor you in all that we do. Amen.

WEEK 25

Dealing with Doubts and Fears

"Peace I leave with you; my peace I give to you. Not as the world gives do I give to you. Let not your hearts be troubled, neither let them be afraid."

John 14:27 (ESV)

Devotion:

As Christian dating couples, we may sometimes struggle with doubts and fears that can threaten to overwhelm us. We may worry about the future of our relationship, about whether we're doing the right things, or about how our lives will unfold. But Jesus offers us a peace that the world cannot give - a peace that can calm our troubled hearts and dispel our fears.

In John 14:27, Jesus tells us, "Peace I leave with you; my peace I give to you. Not as the world gives do I give to you. Let not your hearts be troubled, neither let them be afraid." We can find comfort and strength in these words, knowing that Jesus is with us and that He can give us the peace that we need.

When we face doubts and fears in our dating relationship, let's turn to Jesus and seek His peace. Let's ask Him to help us trust in His goodness and His plans for our lives, even when we can't see the way ahead. And let's remember that we are not alone - that Jesus is with us always, guiding us and comforting us with His love.

PRAYER

Lord Jesus, we thank you for your promise of peace, and your presence with us always. We ask you to help us overcome our doubts and fears and to trust in your goodness and your plans for our lives. Give us the strength and courage that we need to face each day, knowing that you are with us and that your love will never fail. Amen.

WEEK 26

Managing Stress

"Come to me, all who labor and are heavy laden, and I will give you rest."

Matthew 11:28 (ESV)

Devotion:

As Christian dating couples, we face many challenges and responsibilities that can cause us to feel stressed and overwhelmed. Whether it's school, work, family, or other obligations, it's easy to become consumed by the demands of our daily lives.

However, God offers us a solution to the stress and burdens we carry. In Matthew 11:28, Jesus says, "Come to me, all who labor and are heavy laden, and I will give you rest." He invites us to come to Him with our worries, fears, and anxieties, and to find rest in Him.

When we feel stressed, we can turn to God in prayer and ask Him to give us the strength and peace that we need to face our challenges. We can also seek support from our Christian community, whether it's through a small group, church, or trusted friends.

It's important to remember that managing stress is not just about finding ways to cope with it, but also about addressing the root causes of stress in our lives. We can ask God to help us prioritize our time and energy and to show us how to make healthy choices that promote our well-being.

PRAYER

Heavenly Father, we come to you with our stress and burdens. Help us to find rest in you and to trust in your love and care for us. Show us how to make healthy choices that promote our well-being and prioritize our time and energy. Thank You for being our source of strength and peace. Amen.

WEEK 27

Finding Joy in Suffering

"Count it all joy, my brothers, when you meet trials of various kinds, for you know that the testing of your faith produces steadfastness."

James 1:2-3 (ESV)

Devotion:

As Christian dating couples, we will face trials and sufferings in our lives. It can be difficult to find joy in these experiences, but as James 1:2-3 tells us, there is a purpose in our suffering. Trials can test our faith and produce steadfastness within us.

When we face suffering, we can turn to God and ask Him to help us see the purpose in our pain. We can trust that He is working all things together for our good (Romans 8:28), even when it doesn't feel like it in the moment.

We can also find comfort in the fact that we are not alone in our suffering. Jesus Himself endured great suffering on the cross for our sake, and He is with us in our trials. He understands our pain and can sympathize with us (Hebrews 4:15).

Amid our suffering, we can also find opportunities to grow in love and compassion toward others. As we learn to lean on God for strength and comfort, we can be a source of encouragement and hope to those around us who may be going through similar experiences.

PRAYER

Heavenly Father, we know that trials and sufferings are a part of life, but it can be hard to find joy in these experiences. Help us to trust in your goodness and purpose in our pain. Give us the strength to endure and to grow in faith and steadfastness. Help us to be a source of encouragement and hope to those around us who may be going through similar experiences. We trust in your love and care for us. Amen.

WEEK 28

Holding on to Hope

"May the God of hope fill you with all joy and peace in believing, so that by the power of the Holy Spirit you may abound in hope."

Romans 15:13 (ESV)

Devotion:

As we journey through life, we will inevitably face trials and challenges that can cause us to lose hope. It may be a difficult season in our relationship, a job loss, or a health issue. In times like these, it's easy to feel discouraged and lose sight of God's promises.

However, as Christians, we have a hope that is greater than our present circumstances. Romans 15:13 reminds us that God is the "God of hope" who can fill us with joy and peace even amid our struggles. Through the power of the Holy Spirit, we can abound in hope and cling to the promises of God.

Holding on to hope requires an active choice to trust in God's goodness and faithfulness, even when we can't see the way forward. We can turn to God's Word for encouragement and remind ourselves of His promises. We can also surround ourselves with a supportive community of believers who can offer comfort, prayer, and practical help.

PRAYER

Dear God, we thank you for being the God of hope who fills us with joy and peace in believing. Help us to hold on to hope even when we face trials and challenges. Give us the strength to trust in your goodness and faithfulness, and to believe in your promises. Surround us with a community of believers who can offer comfort, prayer, and practical help. Thank You for the hope that we have in you. Amen.

Part Five

God's Plan for Marriage

This part of this devotional series focuses on God's plan for marriage. We will explore the biblical foundations for marriage, the roles and responsibilities of husbands and wives, and the importance of building a Christ-centered marriage. Through these devotionals, we will seek to deepen our understanding of God's design for marriage and apply His principles to our relationships.

WEEK 29

The Purpose of Marriage

"Therefore a man shall leave his father and his mother and hold fast to his wife, and they shall become one flesh."

Genesis 2:24 (ESV)

Devotion:

Marriage is a beautiful and sacred covenant between a man and a woman. It is a reflection of God's love and the union between Christ and His church. Genesis 2:24 tells us that when a man and a woman are joined in marriage, they become one flesh.

The purpose of marriage is to create a lifelong partnership that brings glory to God. It's a relationship that is built on love, commitment, and sacrifice. As spouses, we are called to love and serve one another, just as Christ loved and served us.

Marriage is also a place where we can grow and mature in our faith. It provides us with opportunities to practice forgiveness, humility, and selflessness. As we navigate the ups and downs of life together, we can rely on God's grace and strength to sustain us.

PRAYER

Dear Lord, we thank you for the gift of marriage. Help us to honor you in our relationship and to grow in love and commitment to one another. Teach us to serve each other with humility and selflessness, and to practice forgiveness and grace. We pray that you will bless our marriage and use it to bring glory to your name. Amen.

WEEK 30

Preparing for a Lifelong Commitment

"Commit your work to the Lord, and your plans will be established."

Proverbs 16:3 (ESV)

Devotion:

Preparing for a lifelong commitment is an important step for couples who are considering marriage. It involves more than just planning a wedding ceremony, but also cultivating a strong foundation of faith and trust in God.

Proverbs 16:3 reminds us to commit our work to the Lord, and our plans will be established. This applies not just to our career goals, but also to our relationships. When we commit our relationship to God, we invite Him to be at the center of our decision-making and to guide us as we move forward.

One way to prepare for a lifelong commitment is to spend time in prayer and reflection. We can ask God to reveal any areas of our lives that may need attention and to give us the wisdom and discernment to make wise choices. We can also seek counsel from trusted mentors or Christian counselors who can offer support and guidance.

It's also important to cultivate a strong foundation of trust and open communication in our relationship. This involves being honest with each other about our strengths and weaknesses and being willing to work through challenges together.

As we commit our work to the Lord and prepare for a lifelong commitment, let's remember that our relationship is not just about us, but also about serving and glorifying God. May we trust in His guidance and seek His will for our lives.

PRAYER

Heavenly Father, we commit our relationship to you and invite you to be at the center of our decision-making. Give us the wisdom and discernment to make wise choices and cultivate a strong foundation of faith and trust in you. Help us to communicate openly and honestly with each other, and to work through challenges together. Thank You for guiding us and for your faithfulness to us. Amen.

WEEK 31

Understanding Roles and Responsibilities

"Wives, submit to your own husbands, as to the Lord. For the husband is the head of the wife even as Christ is the head of the church, his body, and is himself its Savior. As the church submits to Christ, so also wives should submit in everything to their husbands."

Ephesians 5:22-24 (ESV)

Devotion:

The concept of submission in marriage can be a challenging one to understand and accept, especially in a culture that values individual autonomy and equality. However, the Bible teaches us that submission is an important aspect of God's design for marriage.

In Ephesians 5:22-24, wives are called to submit to their husbands as to the Lord, just as the church submits to Christ. This does not mean that wives are inferior to their husbands, but rather that they have a unique role and responsibility within the marriage relationship.

As husbands and wives, our roles and responsibilities are different but complementary. Husbands are called to love their wives sacrificially, just as Christ loved the church and gave Himself up for her (Ephesians 5:25). This means putting their needs and interests before their own and seeking to build them up.

As wives, we are called to respect and support our husbands as the leaders of our families. This involves recognizing their God-given authority and following their lead, just as the church follows Christ's lead.

When we understand and embrace our roles and responsibilities in marriage, we can experience greater unity, harmony, and fulfillment. We can work together as a team, each using our unique strengths and gifts to serve one another and glorify God.

PRAYER

Dear God, we thank you for the gift of marriage and for the unique roles and responsibilities that you have given to husbands and wives. Help us to understand and embrace these roles, and to submit to one another out of reverence for you. Give us the strength and wisdom to love and respect one another, and to work together as a team to honor you in our marriage. Amen.

WEEK 32

God's View of Sex and Intimacy

"Let marriage be held in honor among all, and let the marriage bed be undefiled, for God will judge the sexually immoral and adulterous."

Hebrews 13:4 (ESV)

Devotion:

As Christians, we believe that sex and intimacy are a beautiful gift from God that is reserved for marriage. However, in a world that promotes casual sex and glorifies sexual immorality, it can be challenging to maintain a biblical view of sex and intimacy.

Hebrews 13:4 reminds us that marriage should be held in honor by all and that the marriage bed should be undefiled. God has designed sex and intimacy to be a source of joy and intimacy within the context of marriage, and when we honor His design, we can experience the fullness of His blessing.

It's important to remember that our bodies belong to God and that we have a responsibility to honor Him with our choices. As we prepare for marriage or seek to honor God in our current relationships, we can turn to Him for guidance and wisdom.

PRAYER

Heavenly Father, we thank you for the gift of sex and intimacy within the context of marriage. Help us to honor your design and to remember that our bodies belong to you. Give us the strength to resist temptation and to pursue purity in our relationships. Show us how to honor and respect our future spouse or current partner in ways that please you. Thank You for Your guidance and wisdom. Amen.

WEEK 33

Building a Strong Foundation

"Therefore everyone who hears these words of mine and puts them into practice is like a wise man who built his house on the rock."

Matthew 7:24 (ESV)

Devotion:

Building a strong foundation is essential for any lasting and successful relationship. Just as a house needs a solid and secure foundation, our relationships also need a firm groundwork built on godly principles.

In Matthew 7:24, Jesus teaches us the importance of hearing His words and putting them into practice. When we align our relationships with the teachings of Jesus and build our lives on His truth, we establish a strong foundation that can withstand the storms of life.

To build a strong foundation, it's crucial to invest in our spiritual growth individually and as a couple. This means spending time in God's Word, seeking His guidance through prayer, and actively applying His teachings in our daily lives. It also involves cultivating healthy communication, trust, and mutual respect within our relationship.

As we build our relationship on the rock-solid foundation of God's truth, we can face challenges with resilience, experience deeper intimacy, and grow in our love for one another and God.

PRAYER

Dear God, we thank you for the wisdom and guidance found in Your Word. Help us to build a strong foundation for our relationship by aligning our lives with your teachings. Grant us the desire and discipline to invest in our spiritual growth and to apply your truth in our daily lives. May our relationship be rooted in you, and may it bring glory to your name. Amen.

WEEK 34

God's Blueprint for a Healthy Marriage

"Husbands, love your wives, as Christ loved the church and gave himself up for her."

Ephesians 5:25 (ESV)

Devotion:

God's design for marriage is a beautiful and powerful reflection of His love for us. When we follow His blueprint for a healthy marriage, we experience deep connection, intimacy, and joy. One of the most important aspects of a healthy marriage is sacrificial love.

Ephesians 5:25 instructs husbands to love their wives as Christ loved the church and gave Himself up for her. This type of love is selfless, sacrificial, and unconditional. It requires husbands to prioritize the needs, desires, and well-being of their wives above their own. When husbands sacrificially love their wives, they model the love of Christ and create an environment of trust and security in their marriage.

Wives also play an important role in a healthy marriage. In Ephesians 5:22, wives are instructed to submit to their husbands as to the Lord. This type of submission is not about giving up one's autonomy or blindly following a spouse. Instead, it is a willingness to trust and respect one's husband and to work together as a team to build a strong and healthy marriage.

When both spouses are committed to sacrificial love and mutual respect, their marriage becomes a beautiful reflection of God's love for us. As we seek to follow God's blueprint for a healthy marriage, we can trust in His guidance and grace to help us navigate the challenges and joys of married life.

PRAYER

Heavenly Father, thank You for Your design for marriage and the gift of sacrificial love. Help husbands to love their wives as Christ loved the church, and to prioritize their needs, desires, and well-being. Help wives to respect and trust their husbands, and to work together as a team to build a strong and healthy marriage. Guide us as we seek to follow your blueprint for a healthy marriage, and help us to rely on your grace and guidance each day. Amen.

WEEK 35

Leaving and Cleaving

"Therefore a man shall leave his father and his mother and hold fast to his wife, and they shall become one flesh."

Genesis 2:24 (ESV)

Devotion:

Marriage is a sacred covenant between a man and a woman, a joining together of two individuals into one flesh. As couples embark on this lifelong journey together, it is important to understand the principle of leaving and cleaving.

Genesis 2:24 states, "Therefore a man shall leave his father and his mother and hold fast to his wife, and they shall become one flesh." This verse highlights the importance of prioritizing the marital relationship above all other earthly relationships. It calls for a leaving of the dependence on parents and a cleaving, or clinging, to one's spouse.

Leaving and cleaving involve more than just physical separation from parents; it is about establishing a new family unit and a deep emotional bond with one's spouse. It requires a commitment to build a strong foundation for the marital relationship and to prioritize the needs and well-being of one another.

Leaving and cleaving also involves seeking guidance and wisdom from God as the ultimate authority in our lives. As we establish our family unit, we can rely on God's Word to guide us in making decisions, resolving conflicts, and nurturing a healthy and thriving marriage.

Let us embrace the principle of leaving and cleaving in our marriages. May we honor and cherish our spouses, cultivating a relationship that reflects the oneness and unity that God desires for us. Through His grace, may our marriages be a testimony of love, commitment, and faithfulness.

PRAYER

Dear Lord, thank You for the gift of marriage and for the principle of leaving and cleaving. Help us to prioritize our marital relationship and to establish a strong foundation for our family. Help us to rely on you for guidance and wisdom. In Jesus' name, amen.

Part Six

Celebrating Your Love Story

This section is all about reflecting on and celebrating the journey of your marriage. It's an opportunity to look back on all the ways that God has blessed your union and to remember the special moments that have brought you closer together. Whether you've been married for a few months or several decades, taking time to celebrate your love story can be a meaningful way to renew your commitment to each other and God.

WEEK 36

Reflecting on Your Journey

"Let us examine our ways and test them, and let us return to the Lord."

Lamentations 3:40 (ESV)

Devotion:

As we reflect on our journey in marriage, it's important to take time to examine our ways and test them against God's Word. Have we been living according to His will for our lives and our marriage? Have we been loving and serving one another as Christ has called us to do?

It's easy to get caught up in the busyness of life and forget to prioritize our relationship with God and our spouse. But when we take a step back and evaluate our actions, we may realize areas where we need to improve.

Lamentations 3:40 reminds us to examine our ways and test them. This means taking an honest and critical look at our actions and motives and comparing them to God's standards. It also means being willing to make changes and return to the Lord when we have strayed from His path.

Let's take some time to pray and reflect on our journey in marriage. Let's ask God to reveal any areas where we need to improve and give us the strength and wisdom to make changes. Let's commit to living according to His will for our lives and our marriage.

PRAYER

Dear God, we thank you for bringing us together in marriage and for being with us on this journey. As we reflect on our journey, we ask that you would reveal any areas where we need to improve. Help us to examine our ways and test them against Your Word. Give us the strength and wisdom to make changes where necessary, and to live according to your will for our lives and our marriage. We commit our marriage to you, and we ask for your continued guidance and blessing. Amen.

WEEK 37

Recommitting to Your Relationship

"Love one another with brotherly affection. Outdo one another in showing honor."

Romans 12:10 (ESV)

Devotion:

As we journey through life, it's easy to become complacent in our relationships. We get comfortable and forget to put in the effort to show love and appreciation to our spouse. However, just like any other important aspect of our lives, our marriage requires ongoing effort and attention.

Romans 12:10 reminds us to love one another with brotherly affection and to outdo one another in showing honor. This means going above and beyond to demonstrate our love and respect for our spouse. It means taking the time to listen, to be patient, and to show kindness and compassion even when we don't feel like it.

Recommitting to our relationship requires us to be intentional about our actions and words. It means making a conscious effort to prioritize our marriage, to communicate openly and honestly, and to work through any issues or challenges together. We must also be willing to forgive and extend grace to one another as we navigate life's ups and downs.

PRAYER

Dear God, we thank you for the gift of marriage and for the love and companionship that it provides. Help us to recommit to our relationship and to show love and honor to one another. Give us the strength to communicate openly and honestly, and to work through any challenges together. Help us to extend grace and forgiveness to one another as we journey through life. Amen.

WEEK 38

Cultivating Gratitude

"Give thanks in all circumstances; for this is the will of God in Christ Jesus for you."

1 Thessalonians 5:18 (ESV)

Devotion:

Gratitude is an important aspect of any healthy relationship, including marriage. When we cultivate gratitude in our hearts, we are more likely to see the good in our spouse and appreciate the blessings that God has given us. However, it's not always easy to be thankful, especially when we face difficult circumstances.

The Apostle Paul encourages us in 1 Thessalonians 5:18 to "give thanks in all circumstances," recognizing that this is the will of God for us in Christ Jesus. When we choose to give thanks, even amid challenging situations, we are acknowledging that God is in control and that He is working all things together for our good.

Cultivating gratitude requires a deliberate effort to focus on the positive and to look for how God is blessing us. We can start by keeping a gratitude journal, listing the things we are thankful for each day. We can also make a point of expressing our gratitude to our spouse, telling them how much we appreciate them and the ways they bless our lives.

PRAYER

Heavenly Father, thank You for the gift of marriage and for the blessings that You have given us. Help us to cultivate a heart of gratitude, even during difficult circumstances. Teach us to focus on the good and to see your hand at work in our lives. Help us to express our gratitude to our spouse, and to honor and appreciate them in all that we do. Thank You for Your faithfulness and for the many ways that You bless us each day. Amen.

WEEK 39

Remembering Your First Love

"But I have this against you: that you have abandoned the love you had at first."

Revelation 2:4 (ESV)

Devotion:

Marriage is a beautiful gift from God, but over time, the busyness and challenges of life can cause us to lose sight of the love we had at first. We can become so consumed with our daily routines and responsibilities that we forget the passion and excitement we felt when we first fell in love.

In Revelation 2:4, Jesus speaks to the church in Ephesus, saying, "But I have this against you, that you have abandoned the love you had at first." These words also apply to our marriages. We must take time to remember and cultivate the love and passion that brought us together in the first place.

One way to remember our first love is to reflect on our early days together and the things that drew us to each other. We can also make an effort to prioritize quality time together and create new memories that will strengthen our relationship.

Most importantly, we must invite God to be the center of our marriage. When we seek His guidance and direction, we can love each other with a selfless, sacrificial love that reflects the love of Christ.

PRAYER

Dear God, we thank you for the love that brought us together. Help us to remember and cultivate the passion and excitement we felt when we first fell in love. Renew our commitment to each other and to you, and help us to love each other with a selfless, sacrificial love that reflects your love for us. Amen.

WEEK 40

Sharing Your Hopes and Dreams

"For I know the plans I have for you, declares the Lord, plans for welfare and not for evil, to give you a future and a hope."

Jeremiah 29:11 (ESV)

Devotion:

In any marriage, it's important to share hopes and dreams with your partner. When we share our aspirations and desires, we give our spouse a window into our hearts and mind. This creates a sense of intimacy and understanding that can strengthen our relationship.

However, sharing our hopes and dreams also requires vulnerability. It means opening up about our deepest desires and fears and trusting our partner to support and encourage us. This can be difficult, especially if we've been hurt or disappointed in the past.

Yet as Christians, we can find comfort and hope in the knowledge that God has a plan for our lives. Jeremiah 29:11 reminds us that God's plans for us are for our welfare and not for evil, to give us a future and hope. When we share our hopes and dreams with our spouse, we can also trust in God's plan for our lives and our marriage.

PRAYER

Dear God, we thank you for the plans you have for our lives and our marriage. Help us to share our hopes and dreams with one another, and to trust in your plan for our future. Give us the courage to be vulnerable with one another, and the wisdom to support and encourage each other as we pursue our goals. May our relationship be a reflection of your love and kindness. In Jesus' name, we pray, Amen.

WEEK 41

Embracing Your Differences

"For just as the body is one and has many members, and all the members of the body, though many, are one body, so it is with Christ."

1 Corinthians 12:12 (ESV)

Devotion:

Marriage is a union of two individuals who come from different backgrounds, with different experiences and perspectives. It's no surprise that couples may have different preferences, opinions, and ways of doing things. However, instead of seeing these differences as a source of conflict, we can learn to embrace them and see them as a strength in our marriage.

1 Corinthians 12:12 reminds us that just as the body is made up of many parts, each with its unique function, so it is with Christ's body. Similarly, in a marriage, each partner brings their unique qualities, strengths, and weaknesses. When we embrace our differences, we

complement and complete one another, just as the different parts of the body work together.

Embracing differences requires humility, respect, and a willingness to learn from one another. We can seek to understand our spouse's perspective, appreciate their strengths, and support them in areas where they may struggle. When we work together in unity, we can achieve more than we ever could alone.

PRAYER

Dear God, we thank you for creating us with unique qualities and strengths. Help us to embrace our differences in marriage and see them as a strength rather than a source of conflict. Give us humility, respect, and a willingness to learn from one another. May we work together in unity, just as the different parts of the body work together. Thank You for the gift of marriage, and for the ways in which we can complement and complete one another. Amen.

WEEK 42

Planning for Your Future

"But grow in the grace and knowledge of our Lord and Savior Jesus Christ. To him be the glory both now and to the day of eternity. Amen."

2 Peter 3:18 (ESV)

Devotion:

As we plan for our future with our spouse, it's important to remember that our relationship is not just about us. It's about growing in the grace and knowledge of our Lord and Savior Jesus Christ and bringing glory to Him both now and for all eternity.

Growing in grace requires us to constantly seek God's will and wisdom for our lives, and to be open to His guidance and direction. This means setting aside our desires and plans and submitting to God's greater purpose for our marriage.

Growing in knowledge involves deepening our understanding of God's Word and His character, and applying it to our daily lives and our relationship with our spouse. It means committing to ongoing spiritual growth and allowing God to transform us from the inside out.

As we plan for our future, let's recommit to growing in grace and knowledge together as a couple. Let's seek God's will for our lives and our marriage, and trust Him to guide us into the future He has planned for us.

PRAYER

Heavenly Father, we thank you for the opportunity to grow together in grace and knowledge. Help us to always seek your will and wisdom for our lives, and to be open to your guidance and direction. As we plan for our future, help us to trust in your goodness and faithfulness, and to submit our plans to your greater purpose for our marriage. Guide us into the future you have planned for us, and may our marriage bring glory to your name both now and for all eternity. In Jesus' name, Amen.

Takeaway

As we come to the end of this devotional journey on God's plan for marriage, we have explored various aspects of building a strong, healthy, and fulfilling marriage according to God's blueprint. We have learned that marriage is not just a physical and emotional union, but also a spiritual one that requires commitment, sacrifice, and selflessness. We have seen that God's plan for marriage is rooted in love, respect, and mutual submission and that it reflects the relationship between Christ and His church.

But our journey doesn't end here. Marriage is a lifelong commitment that requires ongoing effort, growth, and transformation. As we continue to walk this path together, let us remember the words of 2 Peter 3:18: "But grow in the grace and knowledge of our Lord and Savior Jesus Christ. To him be the glory both now and to the day of eternity. Amen."

Let us continue to seek God's wisdom and guidance for our marriage, and to grow in our love for Him and each other. May we always remember the importance of communication, forgiveness, and grace in our relationship, and may we be willing to put in the work to cultivate a strong and healthy marriage.

PRAYER

Dear God, we thank you for the gift of marriage and for the wisdom and guidance you have provided through this devotional. Help us to apply what we have learned and to continue to grow in our relationship with you and with each other. Give us the strength, patience, and grace to work through the challenges and celebrate the joys of married life. May our marriage be a reflection of your love and may we always give you the glory. In Jesus' name, we pray. Amen.

Made in United States
Troutdale, OR
12/21/2024